Steve Bell & Roger Woddis

Funny Old World

Methuen

Other books by Steve Bell
Maggie's Farm
Further Down on Maggie's Farm
Maggie's Farm - The Last Roundup*
The If... Chronicles*
If... Only Again*
Another Load of If...*
The Unrepeatable If...*
If... Bounces Back*
If... Breezes In*
The Vengeance of If...*
The Revolutionary If...*
If... Kicks Butt*

with Brian Homer
Waiting for the Upturn*

*published by Mandarin

Other books by Roger Woddis
Sex Guyed (with Arthur Horner)
The Woddis Collection
God's Worried

This collection first published in Great Britain
in 1991 by Methuen, Michelin House,
81 Fulham Road, London SW3 6RB

Text copyright © 1988, 1989, 1990, 1991 by Roger
Woddis
Text and Illustrations copyright © 1988, 1989,
1990, 1991 by Steve Bell

The authors have asserted their moral rights

Designed by Brian Homer

Edited by Steve Bell, Roger Woddis,
and Brian Homer

ISBN 0 413 65950 X

A CIP catalogue record for this book is
available from the British Library

Printed and bound in Hong Kong
Produced by Mandarin Offset

All the poems and cartoons in this volume
first appeared in the *New Statesman and
Society*, except the illustrations on pages 1 and
80 which first appeared in *The Guardian*

Contents

Poems by Roger Woddis

Illustrations

See next page

Contents

Illustrations by Steve Bell

Introduction

Believing what your masters tell you can seriously damage your health. All Steve Bell and I, whose work in this book first appeared in the *New Statesman and Society*, can do is warn. Or make you wince. Or possibly even laugh. Our true intent is all for your delight. If we merely pleasure ourselves, we go bland.

All these verses and pictures appeared, more or less in this order, between February 1988 and February 1991. Very often we picked the same subjects - though not necessarily in the same week. Gathered together in this book we believe our words and pictures tell a story. For readers who like to study the historical record the actual dates of original publication are given in the list of contents.

Roger Woddis
May 1991

Anglican Beatitudes

Mrs Thatcher, in private talks with the Archbishop of Canterbury and other senior Church of England bishops, urged them to give a lead in raising 'declining standards of personal morality'

AND spurning the multitudes, she went into private session with her leading prelates:

And she opened her mouth, and taught them, saying,

Blessed are the rich in pocket: for theirs is the freedom of choice.

Blessed are they that screw the poor: for they shall be rewarded.

Blessed are they that pervert the course of justice in the name of national security: for they shall get away with murder.

Blessed are they which do thirst on the Lord's Day: for they shall benefit the brewers.

Blessed are they that kneel to the powerful: for they shall be called my party at prayer.

Blessed are the seekers after perfection: for they shall see Me.

Blessed are the children that die before their time: for they shall save bedspace.

Blessed are the old that die of hypothermia: for they shall save the State money.

Blessed are they which talk of moral values while ripping off the helpless: for theirs is the kingdom of cant.

Let us prey.

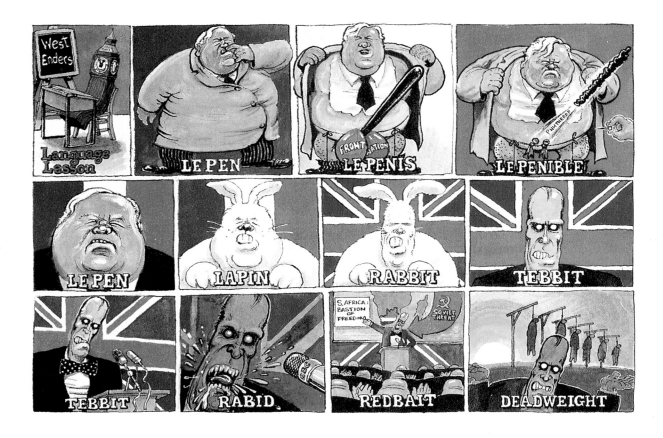

French Kiss

Commentators suggested that Jacques Chirac, the French Prime Minister, had no chance of beating François Mitterrand in the run-off poll for the Presidency unless he accepted the support of the National Front leader, Jean Marie Le Pen

Frère Jacques, Frère Jacques,
Coq or hen, coq or hen?
Is it just a rumour?
Prêtez moi ta plume
Pour Le Pen, pour Le Pen.

Will you welcome, will your welcome
His embrace, his embrace?
Coloured immigration,
African or Asian,
Master-race, master-race.

Down with tyrants, down with tyrants!
Up the poll, up the poll!
D'you remember Neville
Supping with the Devil? –
Oui, c'est drôle, oui, c'est drôle!

Frère Jacques, Frère Jacques,
Not a chance, not a chance.
Mitterrand will make it,
If he doesn't fake it –
Vive la France! Vive la France!

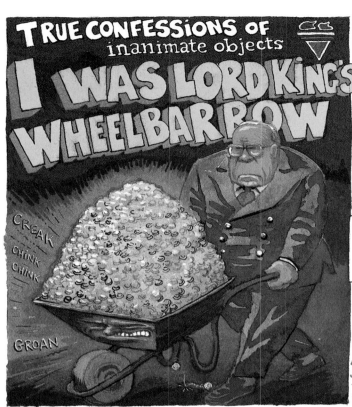

The Heart of Things

'The creation of wealth to me is at the heart of things.' – Mrs Thatcher
'I am not prepared to discuss my personal affairs.'
– Sir Robert Crichton-Brown, outgoing chairman
of Rothmans International, on his retirement gift of
£750,000

God created heaven and earth
And all that in them dwell,
The April showers, the scent of flowers,
The skunks that have a smell.

How well he made, if not a land
That flows with milk and honey,
The musteline whose anal gland
Discharges folding money.

Sir Robert, who would not discuss
His personal affairs,
Will go for gold and thus uphold
The sanctity of shares.

Retirement gifts that trickle down
Increase the widow's mite;
O let us curse the greedy nurse,
And bless the needy knight!

How strange that God, who's in control
And clearly pulls the strings,
Should lose the knack when fuck-you-Jack
Is at the heart of things.

Terminal Case

'How's poor ould Ireland, and how does she
stand?' – old Irish street ballad

The patient lay in a coma,
The doctors stood round the bed,
And many a grave head nodded,
And many a word was said,
And all agreed that the sick one
Was either alive or dead.

But whether they thought the patient
Was dying or merely ill,
They each had the right solution
That either would cure or kill,
With some being keen to move her,
And others to keep her still.

One said, 'Let us change the curtains,'
Another, 'They should be green,'
A third, 'No, I plump for orange –
Or something that's in between.'
Some favoured more drastic measures,
And called for another screen.

They kept under observation
The look of the firm-clenched jaws,
And noted the stertorous breathing,
The bleeding beneath the gauze;
And all of them saw the symptoms,
But none of them knew the cause.

A special nostalgic treat for anyone involved in British Public Life. Take your critical faculty on the holiday of a lifetime in

NORTHERN IRISH HERITAGELAND UK

i internment facility

We've arranged a traditional welcome for you at four in the morning to whisk you away to your carefully chosen camp, just like we did in 1916, 1922, 1938, 1956, and 1971.

A185

Join one of our nostalgia hulks for the voyage of a lifetime, or two years, or six months, or whatever suits your particular lifestyle.

Experienced and courteous security men will conduct you to your quarters.

Wonder at the spectacle of the Protestant Ascendancy and other incredible, unchanging natural phenomena.

Tap your feet and smile as you're denied the right to silence in one of our unique old time Diplock parlours.

Enjoy the best of the old in picturesque combination with the very latest technological developments.

CRUSH DESTROY
RUC-'OUR HANDS ARE TIED IN TERRORIST INTERROGAT'
END THIS RIDICULOUSLY SHORT SENTEN-'ING
Screamer Flash
WE MUST DISCREETLY TAKE OUT THIS EVIL
RUB OUT THE RATS
Bonk
SMASH THIS BRUTALITY
'ULSTER -NEW BATTLE THE ARMY MUST W'N'
EXTINGUISH THESE MURDERERS
Daily Dirt
REVENGE
SEND IN THE SAS TO WIPE THEM OUT
News of the Home Counties
KILL THESE BASTA'
BEAST

Journalists – enjoy the comfort of vigorous ritual denunciation as another young man dies for nothing. Full telephone, telex, fax and broadcasting facilities are available.

TRAVEL BACK IN TIME – TO THE SIX COUNTIES

Eat Your Heart Out Edward Lear!

'We will negotiate with Trident and with the policy line that comes with all that operational weaponry, the policy line that never says yes or no to the question, "Will you press the button?"' – Neil Kinnock

They went to sea in a Sieve, they did,
In a Sieve they went to sea:
In spite of sickness amongst the crew,
And half the passengers wanting to spew,
In a Sieve they went to sea!
And when the Sieve turned round and round,
Everyone feared they'd all be drowned.
And cried as they veered from left to right,
'We won't press the button, then again we
    might!'
In a Sieve we'll go to sea!

Far and few, far and few,
Are the lands where the Fumblies live;
Their heads are pink, and their hearts are blue,
And they went to sea in a Sieve.

They sailed away in a Sieve, they did,
With a compass made of brass;
They tacked in a zigzag policy line,
The course they plotted you could only define
As that of a Whitehall farce.
And everyone said who saw them go,
'They won't say yes, and they won't say no.'
And Neptune said, as he rose from the sea,
'If you like my Trident, please feel free
To stick it up your arse!'

Far and few, far and few,
Are the lands where the Fumblies live;
Their heads are pink, and their hearts are blue,
And they went to sea in a Sieve.

othing

Something for Something

Nothing for Something

Spectrum

The Government learnt, late in the day, that the
environment is a vote-catcher

Red is the colour of desire,
The rebel flag, the forest fire,
The overdraft you may acquire.

Orange the king that some acclaim,
Half of a children's dancing game,
Parties that dare not speak their name.

Yellow denotes a coward's ways,
·The daffodil of distant days,
The warning card the ref displays.

Blue are the eyes we know so well,
The pencil and the Brighton Belle,
The heaven that may turn to hell.

Indigo is a body dye
That ancient Britons would apply:
They called it woad – and scanned the sky.

Violet is a lovely flower
That beautifies a shady bower,
Or shrinking, shows its lack of power.

But what of Green? Let no one speak
Of converts who've a bloody cheek:
Green is the colour of the week.

Rushdie's Baby

Salman Rushdie's apologies for The Satanic
Verses *evoked an emotional response on all sides
and memories of the film* Rosemary's Baby

'I profoundly regret...' He'd caused distress
To followers of Islam who are sincere.
Heaven help him, those were the last words
Some of his best friends wanted to hear.

'How could you Salman?' they cried in pain,
'We, who felt sick to see you banned,
We, who would have been horizontal,
Expected you to make a stand.'

Worse than anything by Polanski,
A book is born – turn up the heat!
Satan's the father of Rushdie's baby!
Look at his eyes – his hands and feet!

The Gotcha! gang, so brave, so pissed,
Howl for the Ayatollah's head.
They're back at base. Fools who are safe
Rush in where Rushdie fears to tread.

Down, they cry, with all mad mullahs!
To hell with killers who read the Koran!
(But not, of course, those splendid fellows
Who enthral Sandy Gall in Afghanistan).

— 'APRIL LOVE' ~

The Sexy Summit

'She looked and sounded like a woman in distinct danger of infatuation.' - the Observer, *on Mrs Thatcher's meeting with Mr Gorbachev*
'All I would ask for is a little bit of balance brought into the debate.' – Hugh Colver, chief spokesman at the Ministry of Defence

Restrain your passion, Madam,
Remember who you are,
The Mother of the Nation,
Our lone and splendid star.
Men lose respect for women
Who let them go too far.

Be guided by Hugh Colver,
Who crawls to serve the State:
A little bit of balance
Brought into the debate
Ensures, along with longing,
A modicum of hate.

Defend your precious honour
Beneath the rising moon,
Resist the red seducer
Who haunts the blue lagoon.
Stand up, stand up for England,
And think of Mills and Boon!

Daniel in the Lioness's Den

President Daniel Ortega of Nicaragua, visiting
Britain on his European tour, met Mrs Thatcher

Do come in, Daniel – mind your feet –
Sorry about these chunks of meat,
They're just ex-ministers' remains,
I had to leave their balls and brains.
You're seeking economic aid
And keen to normalise your trade.
Let us be absolutely frank:
We may have money in the bank,
But when it comes to funds, you know,
Nothing must halt the Contra flow.

What matters to us in the west
Is whether you can pass the test.
We only aid those countries which
Defend the poor against the rich,
Such as South Africa and Chile.
They're run by butchers? – don't be silly,
Death squads protect democracy,
Torture in Turkey shows they're free
And Bush fires prove it most of all.
Bye-bye – so nice of you to call.

Funny Peculiar

'She is going a bit funny.' – Alan Watkins *in the* Observer *on Margaret Thatcher*

This is hardly a laughing matter,
As the lonely traveller said,
When a bird flew out of the turret
And shat on his innocent head.

The lady has been under pressure,
No rival would relish her fate,
Or gentleman think it proper
To query her mental state.

The hand that looked firm now fumbles,
The years have taken their toll,
Pity an ageing Hedda
Who insists on playing the role.

Her name is above the title,
She refuses to leave the scene,
Her eyes see only two colours,
And what isn't red looks green.

Leave her to her delusions,
Like Blanche in the *Streetcar* play,
Who relied on kindness from strangers
When they came to take her away.

"Curses (and turds) are like young chickens, they always come home to roost." (SOUTHEY)

The Scarborough Connection

(After 'The Brook' by Tennyson)
'The subject of water hasn't been handled well or accurately.' – Mrs Thatcher at the 1989 Tory Conference on water privatisation

I come to show you my concern
And end the shilly-shally:
I am not here to twist and turn,
Still less to dilly-dally.

A drink has helped me to relax,
But I am far from tiddly;
I murmur as I raise the axe,
'Good comfort, Master Ridley.'

I may have water on the brain,
I babble of consumers;
You wonder whether I am sane,
I can dispel the rumours.

I chatter madly at the Mace,
No man shall call me coward,
And I can always save my face
By blaming Michael Howard.

I shall pursue my private way,
In spite of public slaughter;
I am quite sure to win in May,
I feel it in my water.

No dam on earth can stop my flow
Or alter my endeavour,
For men may come and men may go,
But I go on for ever.

Double Act

Current opinion polls showed that 90 per cent of West Germans trust Mr Gorbachev in his efforts for peace and disarmament

'Mr Gorbachev,
Oh Mr Gorbachev,
It was *wunderbar* to have you here in Bonn;
We were lavish with our cheers
After sinking several beers,
And we'll still be toasting *glasnost* when
    you've gone.'

'Mr Chancellor,
Oh Mr Chancellor,
I was overwhelmed in Stuttgart and Cologne,
And in Düsseldorf they said
They would welcome me to bed –
It's just as well I wasn't on my own.'

'Mr Gorbachev,
Oh Mr Gorbachev,
You've done wonders for my European poll,
But we'll really paint the town
When the Berlin Wall comes down –
What's to stop you, Mr Gorbachev?'
'Erich Honecker, Herr Kohl.'

The Public Prince

'All the letters sent from my office I have to correct myself, and that is because English is taught so bloody badly.' – Prince Charles

Accustomed as I am to public speaking,
And certain of a sycophantic press,
I knew they wouldn't hesitate in leaking
My latest controversial address.

After my swipe at modern architecture,
Which, so I gather, went down rather well,
I felt that I was qualified to lecture
My subjects on the ghastly way they spell.

What I consider perfectly atrocious
Is correspondence sent on my behalf,
And you will find me at my most ferocious
When publicly belittling my staff.

I blame it all on bloody awful teachers
(Rather than face them, I would cross the road);
One of my best and most endearing features
Is rubbishing the slaves who bear the load.

At Gordonstoun they taught us to be loyal,
To keep a rigid upper and to serve,
Though, frankly, when it comes to being Royal,
One really needs to have a fucking nerve.

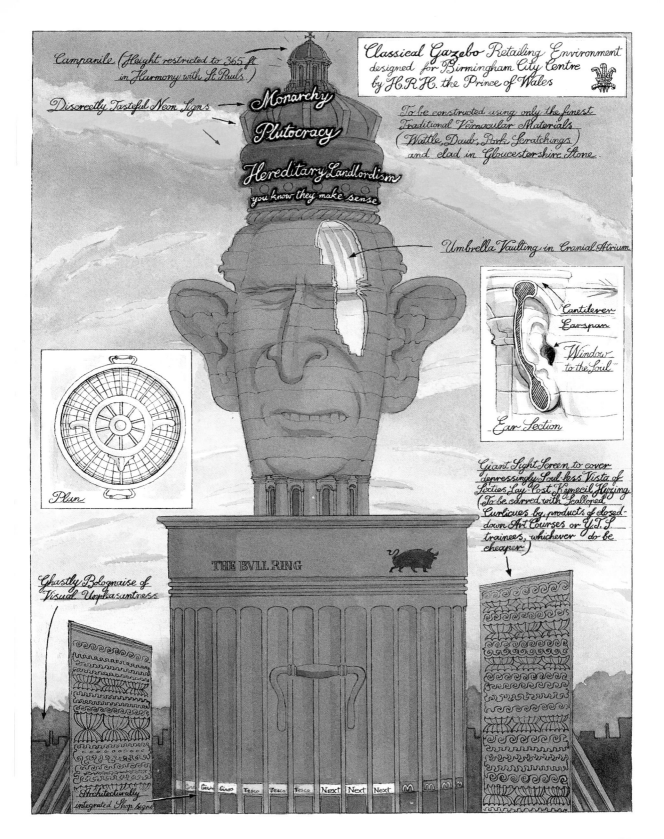

Campanile (Height restricted to 365 ft in Harmony with St Pauls.)

Discreetly Tasteful Neon Signs

Classical Gazebo Retailing Environment designed for Birmingham City Centre by H.R.H. the Prince of Wales

Monarchy
Plutocracy
Hereditary Landlordism
you know they make sense

To be constructed using only the finest Traditional Vernacular Materials (Wattle, Daub, Pork Scratchings) and clad in Gloucestershire Stone.

Umbrella Vaulting in Cranial Atrium

Cantilever Earspan

"Window to the Soul"

Ear Section

Plan

Giant Sight Screen to cover depressingly Soul-less Vista of Sixties Low-Cost Kapecil Huzing (To be carved with Scalloped Curlicues by products of closed-down Art Courses or Y.T.S trainees, whichever do be cheaper.)

THE BVLL RING

Ghastly Bolognaise of Visual Unpleasantness

Architecturally integrated Shop Signs

Advice to the Unborn

You will shortly be entering Britain
Through the usual channel
Without having to produce your papers
Which is something of a rarity.
As someone not unfamiliar with the territory,
I hope you'll find the following helpful.

Don't be born a child. You'll risk
Being abused every which way by your father
Or a family friend or a bewigged buffoon.

Don't be born black, or you'll end up
Black and blue (unless you win and wave
A Union Jack at Gateshead).

Don't be born a woman. You will know,
If your luck holds, a hundred delights,
But you'll have to deal with men.

Don't, when you grow up, do useful work.
Sit at a big desk in the City,
And you'll be laughing.

Don't eat or drink anything at all,
Swim in the sea or live near
A poisonous reactor which is perfectly safe.

If you don't feel up to coping
With these challenges, it might be better
Not to be born at all.

~ The Adoration of the Free Marketised Lamb Product ~

Brush Up Your Polish
or Kiss Me, Katya
(Apologies to Cole Porter)

Brush up your Polish,
Start speaking it now.
Brush up your Polish
And avoid a holy row.
If you can't say Tadeusz Mazowiecki,
Then your future you'd better forgetski.
Just learn to pronounce Lech Walesa,
And they'll think you're a member of Mensa.
You've no role if you're Pole-axed by *zloty*,
Or the Chamber of Commerce is potty.
Brush up your Polish,
And the Pope will bow.

Brush up your Polish,
Start speaking it now.
Brush up your Polish,
Or exams you're sure to plough.
If you wince at Wojciech Jaruzelski,
All the comrades will damn you to hellski,
And whoever misspells Solidarity
Will be greeted by yells of hilarity.
Just remember a Chopin mazurka
Will sound wrong if you rhyme it with
    worker.
Brush up your Polish,
And they'll wreathe your brow.

'AMERICAN SURREAL' or a Right Pair of Bums ———— AFTER GRANT WOOD

Dan, Dan, the Planetary Man

'America's destiny is to discover and to pioneer work in space. We shall keep America first.' – Vice President Dan Quayle, on Voyager II's journey to Neptune

Dan, Dan, the Planetary Man,
More full of wind than a baked beans can,
Sounded off on the theme of space
And the destined role of the master race.

He wrapped himself in the glorious flag,
A bigmouth graduate from Fort Brag.
He swore to defeat corruption and graft,
And avoided colds by dodging the draft.

His eyes were raised to the distant stars,
And he saw them stacked with American cars,
American soaps and American crime,
And preachers selling their souls for a dime.

The future belongs to Planetary Dan,
The mystical, fistical Superman:
Today the world, for better or worse,
Tomorrow the whole Dan universe!

But better not speak in the future tense:
When the sun expands five billion years
    hence,
The earth will explode in a final flash,
Reducing all Quayles to a pile of ash.

Under the Blanket

Lady Chatterley's Lover *was serialised on Radio 4's Book at Bedtime, but a BBC spokeswoman promised that 'sensitive parts would be taken into consideration'*

Times and old usages have changed
Since Lord Reith ran the BBC:
Lost is our sense of innocence,
And so to bed with Lady C.

But Auntie has a rigid rule
(If that's the proper adjective):
Four-letter words should not refer
To parts that may be sensitive.

As prosecuting counsel said,
When D H Lawrence made the news,
'Is this the kind of book you'd wish
Your wife or servant to peruse?'

The Corporation still is pledged
To purge the matter it transmits:
There would be whoops of joy in hell,
If Bromley heard the naughty bits.

Jock Gallagher, the radio head,
Stands guard on decency and taste,
And has imposed a blanket ban
On certain acts below the waist.

The goings-on at Wragby Hall
Are far too rude for Radio 4.
It is your Christian task to kill,
And wicked to make love, not war.

Panic

After 'Nerves' by Sagittarius, a famous New Statesman *satirist, who voiced her anxieties on the eve of World War Two in September 1939 and inspired these lines on the economy fifty years later*

I think I'll get a paper,
I think I'll watch the news.
I need to know what's going on,
I'm running out of booze.

It's just like that October
The year before the last.
I think I'll play some Haydn
Until the storm has passed.

I'll ask my local bookie,
He's sure to know what's what.
I'll ring the Bank of England,
I think I'd better not.

I think I'll read a thriller
Or a Mills and Boon romance.
I think I'll look at *Question Time*,
I think I'll fill my pants.

They say it won't affect us,
They say perhaps it will.
They say the market's healthy.
I wish I weren't so ill.

They're going to raise my mortgage
They're calling in the loans.
I wonder what the FT thinks,
And who the hell's Dow Jones?

I can't imagine what effect
These experts that you see
Will have upon our enemies,
But God, they frighten me.

THE MAN WHO SUGGESTED THE DISTANT HYPOTHETICAL POSSIBILITY OF A POLITICAL SETTLEMENT IN NORTHERN IRELAND

TRIUMPHANT VINDICATION OF BRITISH JUSTICE

AFTER PIRA

Tipping the Scales

Irish 'terrorists', known as the Guildford Four, were released in 1989 after fifteen years' wrongful imprisonment

They call it a crime and a scandal,
They say it's a sin and a shame,
And banging up innocent people
Gives criminal law a bad name.
All right, if we'd hung onto hanging,
It's likely they'd not be alive;
They talk about fifteen years wasted,
But what of the Guildford Five?

I'm talking of hard-working coppers,
The bravest and best of the force.
True-blue and sincerely believing
A fit-up is par for the course.
The victims are quickly forgotten,
Now where is the fairness in that?
Lose sleep over Carole and Gerard,
Or weep for a Paul or a Pat?

Suppose we uncovered corruption
And dug up a dead DPP,
Or questioned the word of our masters,
Where would democracy be?
Its very foundations would crumble
And rubble be left of the bricks,
If, heaven forbid, they reopened
The case of the Birmingham Six.

"Up Shit Creek"

When

(After Kipling's If*)*
Following the resignation of Nigel Lawson as Chancellor of the Exchequer, Tory MPs were openly expressing alarm at their leader's waning popularity

When you have lost your head and all about
   you
Are shaking theirs and looking worried stiff,
When even erstwhile cronies want to clout
   you,
And wonder when you will depart, not if,
When you are too grotesque for *Spitting Image,*
And only the weak-minded think you strong,
When you emerge unruffled from the
   scrimmage,
But leave behind a godalmighty pong.

When all your slaves once willing to oblige'll
Refuse to do your bidding and resign;
When lower ranks, resolved to follow Nigel,
Vote with their feet and leave the thin blue
   line.
When all the polls reveal your stock is
   slipping,
When members voice their anguish over tea,
And none of them is eager for a whipping,
Still less to end their days like Blore, MP:

When, like the House of Usher, but much
   faster
Than anything in Edgar Allan Poe,
Your reign collapses in the last disaster,
And all the nation cries, 'For God's sake, go!'
When Walden stops you in the final minute,
And only you pretend that you have won,
But know full well that you are deeply in it,
Then even you must know your day is done.

After the Wall

After the Wall had crumbled,
After the East strolled through,
Warriors ran for cover,
Wondering what to do.
Many a giant bogey
Suddenly looked quite small.
Many went mad in the media
After the Wall.

Who will end up the loser?
Who is it stands to win?
Questions like soaring eagles
Hover above Berlin.
Prophets who fear the future
Peer at their crystal ball,
Chickens run round with their heads off
After the Wall.

Germany reunited,
Threats of a master race –
If Egon Krenz is ousted,
Will it be Egon Face?
Nutters and friends of Nato
Issue a frantic call:
'How can we live without hatred? –
Bring back the Wall!'

Polar Bears in Piccadilly

'It is impossible to prove that the alliance structure is the reason for Europe's long spell of peace since 1945, but it seems a safe assumption ... we should be in no hurry to bury Nato.' – Nigel Hawkes in the Observer

People know, who study logic,
One of life's most basic laws:
What precedes a certain outcome
May not be its primal cause.
As they say in classic Latin,
Post hoc, ergo propter hoc,
Or, to put it more precisely,
Nigel Hawkes is talking cock.

'Don't be quick to bury Nato,'
Warns our Diplomatic Ed.
'If it weren't for paranoia,
You and I would both be dead.'
Once a man in Piccadilly,
Firing wild, was heard to say
Shooting off in all directions
Kept the polar bears away.

'Polar bears in Piccadilly?
Never!' said a passer-by.
'Proves my point – it's damned effective,'
Was the hawkish one's reply.
Such apparent lack of reason
Filled his hearers with alarm.
Those in white who knew the symptoms
Took him gently by the arm.

The Knife of Brian

Norman Tebbit, Lord (Woodrow) Wyatt and other
notable right-wingers accused the BBC of anti-
government bias, and called for the dismissal of
Brian Redhead

Brian, Peter, Sue and John
Go to work with their blinkers on.
So, at least, some people say
Who simply cannot stand *Today*.

While sleepy Britons sweat and snore,
The keenest wake to Radio 4,
Uncaring that at half-past six
The Beeb begins its knavish tricks.

How many listeners suss the plot
Devised by Redhead and his lot,
And realise the morning news
Is poisoned with subversive views?

They use the word 'Conservative'
The way that Mack employed a shiv.
There are demands to stop the show –
Brian the Knife will have to go!

To blow one's top and raise a storm,
When you are losing, is the Norm.
Though only weatherfolk are free
From bias on the BBC.

Tears at No. 10

(Apologies to Cole Porter, and to Ella Fitzgerald)
Peter Walker, the former Welsh Secretary, who
resigned from the Government, was the third
minister to leave in six months

Every time we say goodbye
I die a little,
Every time we say goodbye
I wonder why a little,
Why the sods who leave me
Don't care, though once devout,
How much it will grieve me
If they all Peter out.

At the start, they seemed to share
My way of thinking;
Rats depart, when they're aware
The ship of state is sinking.
There's no team stronger,
But I fear
It's clear
I won't last much longer,
Every time they say goodbye.

Patrick James Hill   Hugh Daniel Callaghan   John Walker   Richard McIlkenny   William Power   Robert Gerard Hunter

OLD SCAPEGOATS

I SEE BY YOUR UNIFORM AND/OR PRIVILEGED NON-IRISH BACKGROUND THAT YOU HAVE BEEN PUNISHED ENOUGH

Mr Justice, now Lord Donaldson (Guildford Four trial judge)   Mr Justice, now Lord Bridge (Birmingham Six trial judge)   Lord Denning, former Master of the Rolls   Chief Justice Lord Lane   Late Chief Justice Lord Widgery   Mr Justice Class-Bias

OLD GOATSCAPE

Guilty as Framed

Granada Television broadcast a programme on the Birmingham pub bombings of 1974

Our native urge to see fair play
Makes Britain what she is today:
Although the flag of truth stays furled,
We are the wonder of the world.

Long after the horror, everyone
Still mourns the murdered 21.
We may, sir, have misjudged the Six,
But after all, that's politics.

Let no one vilify Lord Lane,
Or in their innocence complain
That treatment meted out was rough.
These men are Irish. That's enough.

The Lord Chief Justice, bless his wig,
Thinks being wrong is infra dig
And slumbers peacefully at night,
Knowing the law is always right.

The Ballad of Britain's Jails

(With apologies to Oscar Wilde)
After the prison riot at Strangeways in 1990
(under Governor Brendan O'Friel) the then Home
Secretary, John Waddington, set up an enquiry
chaired by Lord Justice Woolf

I never saw a man who looked
    So broken on the wheel,
Or tortured on a rack of pain
    As Governor O'Friel,
Like one who wakes from dreadful dreams
    And finds them all too real.

Yet each man hates the job he does,
    Of that there is no doubt:
Some weep about their woeful pay,
    Some climb the roof and shout,
The warder stressed by stopping in,
    The convict slopping out.

I know not whether Waddington
    Has work beyond his range;
All that I know is that the ways
    Of God and Man are strange,
And that there is no unjust law
    That crying 'Woolf' will change.

The vilest crimes of modern times,
    Some say, deserve the 'cat',
But he who thinks the system soft
    Is talking through his hat.
Better show *Porridge* once again,
    And make us laugh at that.

One Man's Meat

(Acknowledgments to G K Chesterton)
Faced with EEC condemnation of UK
slaughterhouses for their filthiness, a meat trade
spokesman said, 'We are going to carry on putting
shit on our meat until the housewife objects'

God made the British butcher
   For a mystery and a sign,
That carnivores might praise the Lord
   When they sit down to dine;
And whether roasted, grilled or stewed,
   Or skewered on a spit,
They thank Him for their daily bread
   When they are eating shit.

The meat that fills your burgers,
   Your sausages and pies,
Has been befouled by faeces
   And crawled upon by flies;
This hardly shakes the housewife,
   But shocks the EEC,
Which makes the meat trade wonder,
   How fussy can you be?

Our British slaughterhouses,
   Where filth lies inches thick,
Make foreigners refuse our meat
   And say it makes them sick;
But they forget who damn us
   (O! our offence is rank!)
That one man's poison to another
   Is money in the bank.

— DIFFICULTIES WITH READING —

Funny You Should Say That

'A good sense of humour will not go amiss ...
equally important, though, is a strong
imagination.' – Teacher recruitment advert by the
Department of Education and Science

Looking for secure employment?
Want a job that's free from stress,
One that offers pure enjoyment?
Come and join the DES.

All you need is dedication,
As requested in our ad,
Plus a strong imagination.
(Even better if you're mad.)

Why end up a starving beggar?
Be a teacher! – go for gold!
Follow jolly John Macgregor,
Swallow everything you're told.

Never mind the cuts and capping,
You're the kind we hope to kid.
(Telly plugs and fancy wrapping
Only cost two million quid.)

Though complaints on pay and status
May be voiced among the staff,
Even malcontents who hate us
Must admit we raise a laugh.

Lord Cable

Who worked tirelessly in the service of his country,
and thereby did himself a Power of Good
(Verses inspired by events following the
resignation of Lord Young as Secretary to the
Department of Trade and Industry)

Lord Cable seemed by nature made
To work in Industry and Trade.
Whatever circumstance befell,
His Lordship served his country well,
Without, I hasten to explain,
A single thought of Private Gain.

In time he left the DTI,
And sadly, as he dabbed his eye,
He said, 'It breaks my heart to go,
But I am needed, as you know,
To chair a Certain Board, and gosh,
They've offered me a lot of Dosh.'

His going left a nasty taste,
And some said, 'What Indecent Haste!
How can the Government now rage
At those who want a living wage?'
Lord Cable told them, 'I'm the Boss,
And frankly, I don't give a Toss.'

Last Resort

Military establishments in the Soviet Union, the US and Britain expressed anger at the arms cuts proposed by both East and West

In some secluded hideaway,
    Remote from prying eyes,
Three mad bemedalled generals
    With brains of massive size
Stared dumbly at the dreadful news,
    And felt their hackles rise.

One chewed the end of his cigar,
    And one began to sweat,
The third remarked, 'Of all the foes
    That we've confronted yet,
The loss of status, power and pay
    Remains the greatest threat.'

The thought of peace disturbed them all;
    And filled them with alarm:
'Let's stage an international coup -
    We're done if they disarm.'
But that's the kind of talk you hear
    In any funny farm.

Half an Eye

Violence erupted in Trafalgar Square during an anti-Poll Tax demonstration in 1990

Nelson, silent on his column,
Gazed upon the scene below,
Sickened by the rival forces
Who were trading blow for blow.
Briton fighting fellow Briton
Filled him with a dark despair,
And the lions wept on seeing
Bloodshed in Trafalgar Square.

Burning, looting, shattered windows,
Acts beyond all human sense,
Joy of anarchists and vandals
Jerking off on violence,
Helpless hands held up in horror,
Purblind leaders asking, 'Why?'
What escapes their narrow vision
Nelson sees with half an eye.

Blame it on the opposition,
Muddy what is crystal-clear;
Any stick to beat a dog with,
Any chance to spread a smear.
Blame the marchers, blame the media,
Blame the weather, blame the blacks,
Blame whatever comes in handy
Blame them all – but not the tax.

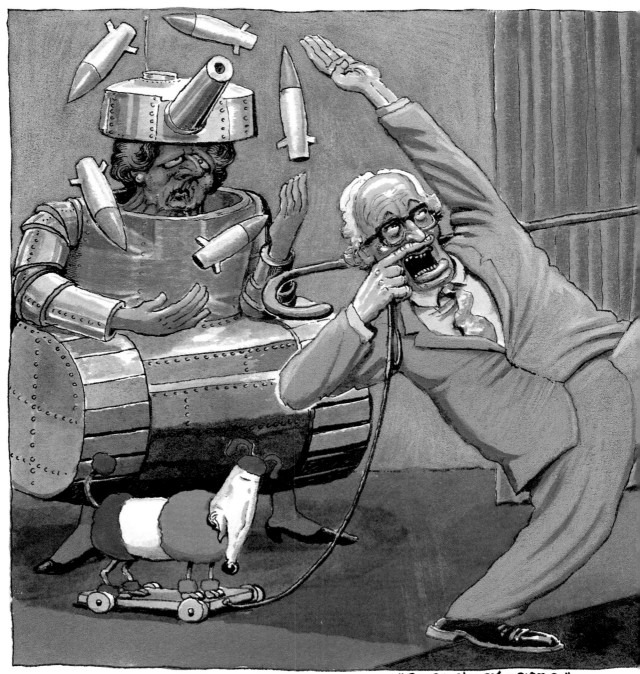

"GO·GO RIDLEY – PART 2"

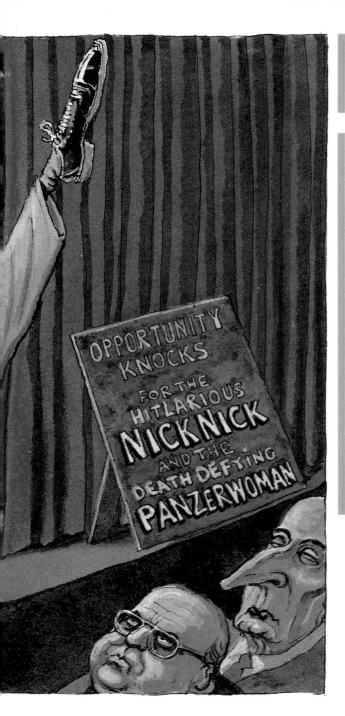

Don't Let's Be Beastly to Nick Ridley

(With apologies to Noël Coward)
Trade Secretary Nicholas Ridley's anti-German stance led to his resignation in July 1990

Don't let's be beastly to Nick Ridley,
Who expressed unbridled hatred for the Hun,
Though he used the kind of language
Every diplomat deplores,
He was only playing *forte*
What is felt by Her Indoors.
Let's all rise to him,
When waving our goodbyes to him,
And weep when he fires the suicidal gun.
Let's treat the chap with charity,
Regretting his vulgarity,
But don't think that he's the only one.

Don't let's pretend the man was tiddly,
Or suggest his ghastly gaffe was all in fun.
If his words had been more measured,
As he readily admits,
He'd have not dismayed the Government
And given them the shits.
Wave a flag for him,
And light another fag for him,
Denying his awful blunder takes the bun.
Let's weigh the gain and loss in it,
And say he's dropped the Boss in it,
But don't rubbish Labour's favourite son.

Look Who's Talking

'This repulsive charade takes to new extremes the hypocrisy of Saddam Hussein and his callous disregard for human rights and individual feelings.' – A Foreign Office spokesman on the Saddam TV spectacular during the Gulf crisis

Oh, horror! What a ghastly show!
The man is evil, as we know,
But looking at his oily smile
(So typical of Arab guile),
One could not fail to apprehend
This rotter really is the end.
What cant! What shameless tommyrot!
It turns one's stomach, does it not?

We in the Foreign Office shrink
From propaganda ploys that stink,
And never turn off all the lights
Till we've secured all human rights.
One must make clear that one detests
His dubbing hostages as 'guests'.
(It's quite some time, when all is said,
Since we were patting Saddam's head.)

To fend off critics who attack,
The kettle calls the teapot black,
But who's to say, 'What bloody cheek!'
Humbug is flavour of the week.
Our solemn duty is to hate
The murderers that we create:
As Frankenstein remarked, 'Good God!
My monster's joined the awkward squad!'

PowerGen to the People

'There will be no sweeteners, there will be no secret deals, and, at this moment, there is no deal at all.' – John Wakeham, the Energy Secretary on the privatisation of the electricity industry

No one should cast aspersions,
No one should talk of sleaze,
No one should say he's full of bull,
The way a dog has fleas.

No one should shift the bedrock
The castle's built upon
By shouting 'Shame!' at Hanson,
Or doubting Honest John.

No one should cry corruption,
Or hint at secret deals,
No one should lift the loo-lid
And see what it reveals.

No one should think, who finds it hard
To live on what they earn,
That paying into Tory funds
Ensures a fat return.

No one should weep or lose much sleep
When Britain's up for sale,
Or question why it's lords who laugh,
And thieves who go to jail.

No one should say it's private gain
That poisons public life,
Or think our green and pleasant land
Is run by Mack the Knife.

Brave Music, Distant Drums

Mark Elder was sacked as conductor from the last night of the Proms by John Drummond, controller of Radio Three, for refusing to conduct jingoistic songs during the Gulf crisis

Land of Hope and Glory,
Mother of the Free,
How shall we extol soldiers
Sent across the sea?
Sailors nurtured on Nelson,
Lovely lads dropping bombs,
Can't compare with the people
Queuing for the Proms.

Singing *Rule, Britannia*
Stirs the coldest heart;
Men who march together
Soon are blown apart.
God who made thee mighty,
Make thee mightier yet;
Medal-winners remember,
Music-lovers forget.

Stamp your feet *fortemente,*
Wave those Union Jacks;
Promenaders sing jingo,
Elder leans towards *pax.*
Elgar rouses John Drummond,
Parry means a packed hall;
Troops who die for their country
Tend to sing *Fuck 'em all.*

The Sick Child and the Bumptious Adult — after Edvard Munch.

The Mask of Clarkery

(After 'The Mask of Anarchy' by Shelley)
Kenneth Clarke, when Health Secretary, attacked
the ambulance workers' overtime ban for
'threatening patients'

I met Ordure in the park –
He had a mask like Kenneth Clarke –
Glib of tongue and round of limb,
Seven cameras followed him.

Fiercely he condemned the ban
(Is this a robot or a man?);
And spoke with passion of a threat
By those eternally in debt.

From his eyes large teardrops fell
For all the injured and unwell;
They flooded his official car
And put an end to his cigar.

Though not inclined to waste his breath
On those who daily deal with death,
He feared one shift spent at the face
Would make of him a stretcher-case.

And while he wept for those in pain,
The greatest threat, he now made plain
To all except the deaf and blind,
Came from Ordure and his kind.

Rise like lions after slumber,
Now that you have got his number;
Shake the mask from creatures who
Shed huge tears and sicken you.
We are many - they are few.

By Way of an Emetic

(Apologies to Edward Lear)
*'We have never given, and will never give support
of any kind to the Khmer Rouge.' - Foreign
Secretary Douglas Hurd, quoted by John Pilger, in
his ITV report on Cambodia*

How pleasant to know Mr Hurd!
A civilised chap through and through:
He never would utter a word,
Unless it were totally true.

Whenever he ventures to speak,
He displays a remarkable knack
For keeping his tongue in his cheek,
And two fingers crossed at his back.

At plying his trade he is skilled,
He is honest and freedom's custodian.
(Unless you should chance to be killed,
And happen to be a Cambodian.)

He has a most flexible mind,
He claims to be nobody's stooge,
And thinks it unfair and unkind
To hint that he backs the Khmer Rouge.

He castigates Saddam Hussein,
But denies that he has a soft spot
For licensed purveyors of pain,
Or prays every night for Pol Pot.

His media detractors are few,
He weeps for the World that is Third;
And if you are ready to spew,
How pleasant to know Mr Hurd!

Not one of us

Canon Eric James stopped his regular contributions to Thought for the Day on BBC Radio 4's Today programme because of censorship, notably of a script about John Groser, the radical London priest, on the opening day of the Labour Party conference

Where are the priests who simply prayed?
The Beeb is now bereft of them.
What trouble radicals have made!
How devilishly deft of them!
All honour to the right brigade,
With canons to the left of them.

The so-called man of God who claims
To serve the needy and the sick
Should go to hell and feed the flames,
To save the body politic.
Behind the mask of Canon James,
Behold a crypto-Bolshevik.

John Groser loved the human race
And thought their needs were paramount;
And Eric, too, to his disgrace,
Believes the common people count.
They want no priests at Portland Place
Who preach the Sermon on the Mount.

Now he is gone, let us rejoice
By sending up a hymn to Her,
Who has declared her faith in choice
And knows that listeners prefer
A vicar with a plummy voice
To some subversive carpenter.

Letters Patent

According to a Dutch newspaper, British soldiers in the Gulf invented a new use for condoms, supplied free by Virgin, as covers for their guns to keep the sand out

When Tommy humps his heavy gear
To hot spots on the map,
It isn't thoughts of *bint* and beer
That motivate the chap:
Whatever stories you may hear
The Dutch are sure to cap.

We know each squaddie over there
Who's sweating in the sun
Will brave the worst and do and dare,
Until the battle's won,
And will protect, with rubberware,
The barrel of his gun.

Your Virgin soldier's one desire
Is to defeat the sand,
And for this purpose will acquire
Whatever comes to hand:
His weapon must be sure to fire,
If he's to make a stand.

His story may be short, and end
In glory or a wreath,
And though survival may depend
On God and Edward Heath,
At least he knows the soldier's friend
Is safe within its sheath.

~ THE GOLDEN SCENARIO ~

A Shropshire Lass

(On the anniversary of the death of A E Housman)
'She remains fit and energetic, and has created the
impression that she will fight room by room to
remain in Downing Street' - *the* Observer

Looniest of all, the Lady now
Ignores the gloom on every brow,
And brushes anxious friends aside,
Who think she should be certified.

Now, of her threescore years and five,
Eleven will, with luck, survive
As years when thousands garnered more
And millions hammered on her door.

And though observers now assume
That she will fight from room to room,
As May will prove and drinkers know,
When bladders burst, you have to go.

Thursday Bloody Thursday

(After 'Bredon Hill' by A E Housman)
Labour retained their seats at two key by-elections
in November 1990

In Bradford North and Bootle,
Where bells ring loud and clear,
The Tory faithful gather,
As polling day draws near,
And shit themselves with fear.

And there this Thursday morning,
When omens fill the sky,
Their thoughts will be of Geoffrey,
With Douglas standing by
And Michael riding high.

And they will hear the goddess
In London far away:
'Come worship me my darlings.'
But none will kneel to pray
Who see her feet of clay.

And some will be obedient,
And some will disagree,
Remembering what happened
To those who bent the knee
To Rider Haggard's *She.*

In Bradford North and Bootle,
Where devotees look glum,
The Mother of the Nation
Is slow to grasp why some
No longer lick her bum.

~ The Stalking Sheep ~

AFTER HOLMAN HUNT 'THE SCAPEGOAT'

Cinderella '91

A Classless Pantomime

Characters

Cinderella	*working girl*
Lady Margaret	*an ex-Leader*
Sir Denis	*a sort of baronet*
Mark	*their favoured son*
Carol	*their freelance daughter*
Boyo	*a freckled buttons*
Fairy Godmother	*a figment of the media*
Prince Michael	*an ambitious jerk*
Johndini	*a minor-domo*

Act 1 Scene: *A kitchen in Dulwich. Cinderella discovered, sweeping.*

Cinderella I clean and scrub and slave all day,
I work long hours for lousy pay,
When things go wrong, I get the blame:
I might as well be on the game.

Lady M *(entering)*
Stop slacking! Get your finger out!
Why do I have to scream and shout
To motivate the working class?
Be proud of Britain! Shift your arse!
Remove that rubbish! Fill that pail!

Cinderella Tote that barge and lift that bail.

Lady M How shocking! Are you mocking me?

Cinderella Hooray for high society!

Lady M Society? There's no such thing –

Cinderella Apart from Louis, Frank and Bing.

(enter Mark and Carol)

Mark We've been invited to the ball
They're holding at Westminster hall!

Carol It's from Prince Michael -

Lady M – what, of Kent?

Carol No, mumsy – the Environment,
You know, the one who nicked the mace.

Lady M The bastard tried to take my place!
Because of him, I lost my crown.

Cinderella That's why, stepmother, you stepped down.

Mark Be quiet, Cinders – belt up do!
The Prince is not inviting *you*.

Cinderella I'd give my pussy to be there,
But I don't have a thing to wear –
Besides, they'd never let me in.

Sir Denis *(entering)*
Has anybody seen the gin?

Lady M It's far too early, don't you think,
For even you to have a drink?

Sir Denis We ought to celebrate, my pet –
I've just been made a baronet!
And you're now Mrs T, OM!

Lady M Whatever has come over them?
I am a *tigress*, not a cat!
A fiery *female* autocrat!

Sir Denis Not 'Tom', dear, it's the Order of
Merit.

Mark Congratters, Dad. Will I inherit
Your title when you meet your
God?

Sir Denis You can't wait, can you? you little
sod.

Carol And I'll be Lady Carol – wow!

Mark Oh no, you won't, you stupid cow,
That's not the way the line
descends.

Carol Oh, well, I always have *Loose Ends*.

Lady M I must get dressed - tonight will be
A photo opportunity.

(they exit, leaving Cinderella)

Cinderella I'm lonelier than you suppose.

Boyo *(entering)*
You've still got Boyo – have a rose.
I represent the talking class.

Cinderella You're boring - but we'll let it pass.

How do I get to meet the nobs,
Who never do the dirty jobs?

*(Lady M re-enters as Fairy Godmother,
wearing OM badge)*

Fairy Godmother
It's easy – wish upon a star,
Follow the *Sun* and you'll go far.

Cinderella I thought they'd given you the
sack.

Fairy Godmother
And so they did - but know I'm
back,
And still our country's favourite
blonde.
I can do wonders with my wand -
A pumpkin coach and horses, too,
Are guaranteed by voting blue.

Cinderella Well, blow me down! What can
this mean?

Boyo A Major transformation scene!

Curtain

Act 2 Scene: Outside the Palace of
Westminster. Enter Cinderella and Boyo.

Cinderella How do you like the way I'm
dressed?
Will Tarzan think I pass the test?

Boyo He'll tell you, 'You're not one of
us,
You've just come off the Clapham
bus',
But seeing how he's missed the
boat,
He'll do his nut to get your vote.

(enter Prince Michael)

Cinderella Prince Michael – should I call you
'sir'?

P Michael PM, is what I'd much prefer.
I know we've never met before,

But will you join me on the floor?
We could discuss the passing
show,
And why the poll tax has to go.

Cinderella Action's what's needed, talk is
cheap.
(aside) Me, Cinderella - you, a
creep.

(they exit)

Boyo I hope they're dancing far apart –
Oh, for a chance to win her heart!
I'll nab her, or my name's not Neil,
By endless chat and sex appeal.

(enter Johndini)

Johndini I am the minor-domo here,
I offer hope and bring good cheer
By promising to make things hum,
With lots of lovely things to come.

Boyo/Johndini *(together)*
We may seem rivals, but we're
twinned,
And both of us are piss and wind.

Johndini I came, I saw, I conquered Rome –

Boyo It's past my bedtime. Who goes
home?

(Big Ben strikes)

Cinderella *(entering)*
The clock is striking twelve – oh
hell!
My deadline's due! God help Steve
Bell!
If I should fail in meeting it,
The rest of us are in the shit!

(she exits)

Johndini I see she's left her glove behind –
I mustn't **** or I'll go blind.

Boyo All problems will be solved in time
If you believe in Pantomime!

Curtain

Act 3 Scene: *The Dulwich Kitchen. Enter the
Prince, Cinderella and Boyo.*

Prince M I'm looking for a likely wench,
Prepared to join me on the bench,
Who backs the policies I've
planned -
Now come on, Cinders, show
your hand.

Cinderella The glove you offer doesn't fit,
Your lot will not get rid of it.

Boyo Allow me, sir – please let me try,
I am prepared to do or Dai.
I'd rubbish Roy or banish Benn,
If I could get to Number Ten.

Cinderella I never thought that you were gay.

Boyo I'm not, my dear, but who's to say
What Labour leaders will not do
To bend the knee to You-know-
who?

(Boyo tries on glove)

Prince M   It fits, it fits! This must be love!

Boyo   It isn't, but we're hand in glove.
         Although it's true we've never
           kissed,
         It pays to be a pragmatist.

(enter Sir Denis and Lady Margaret)

Cinderella Whatever's wrong? You look so
           pale.

Sir Denis We're putting Dulwich up for sale.

Lady M   We've exercised our right to
          choose.

Cinderella Well, some you win, and some you
          lose.
Sir Denis Chelsea will cost nine million quid,
         And no one will exceed our bid.

Lady M   But Cardboard City's moving in!

Sir Denis I think I need a double gin.
         Our era's over – where's the fizz?

Lady M   Oh, no, it's not!

Cinderella Oh, yes, it is!
         It's all in *Old Moore's Almanack:*
         Farewell the age of fuck-you-Jack!

Final Curtain

Labels within cartoon:
OIL SPECULATOR LOSES SHIRT
SADDAM WITHDRAWS FROM KUWAIT
LOCAL CATS DISCOVER NEWSNIGHT SANDPIT
OIL PRICE PLUMMETS
FREE GALLON WITH EVERY GLASS
THE "NIGHTMARE SCENARIO"
© Steve Bell '90

Such a Lust

'What disposes the Anglo-Saxons to such a lust for
bigger bangs?' – Edward Pearce in The Guardian

When this lovely war is over,
Oh, how wretched we shall be!
When our boys have gone to glory,
No more talkathon TV,
No more bull from General Blackhead,
No more hymns to British phlegm,
No more telling tearful widows
What our lads have done to *them*.

When this war for Truth and Freedom
Ends in victory for the west,
We can turn to graver matters,
Such as why we lost the Test.
No more flaky air vice-marshals
Getting off on former prangs,
No more lunatics displaying
Such a lust for bigger bangs.

When they finish with the phone-ins,
When the blood has ceased to flow,
No more lying politicians,
No more bilge from Peter Snow.
When you tire of seeing children
Begging for a bowl of rice,
Think of those who, flogging weapons,
Pray for war at any price.

The Show Mustn't Go On

(With apologies to Noël Coward)
Party Night at the Adelphi Theatre in celebration
of the Labour Party was abandoned because of 'the
present situation in the Gulf'

Only the Master
Could sing of disaster
And bring us delight,
But clowns with red noses
And sporting red roses
Just doesn't seem right.
Pity about the show they banned,
Think of the throngs along the Strand,
If Madame Arcati
Had roused the whole party
To put up a fight
Next Sunday night.

I'd banked on a marvellous party
For Boyo and Hatters and co,
Full of music and wit,
But I wanted to spit
When I learnt that they'd cancelled the show.
But one shouldn't damn the poor darlings
For boldly supporting the war;
When braver believers
Are burning their boats,
You might blame our leaders
For turning their coats
And selling their souls
To secure a few votes,
But that's what the party's for.

Right Reverend

'We cannot allow the high human cost of war totally to inhibit the use of armed force against aggressors.' – Richard Harries, Bishop of Oxford

When ancient cities disappear,
And half the Holy Land is gone,
We shall be urged to raise a cheer
For Christian soldiers marching on.

The bad shall perish by the sword,
And if this leads to genocide,
We can rely upon the Lord
To say our cause is justified.

It is a sin to love your foe,
And wrong to turn the other cheek:
The pet we patted years ago
Became a hound from hell last week.

A British pilot may be lost,
An Arab child may lose a limb;
The faithful will not count the cost,
Their duty is to worship Him.

When comes the happy hour to strike,
And Baghdad's coupled with Cape Cod,
Muslim and Christian priest alike
Shall grovel to a gung-ho God.

Forgetting what is in the Book,
Regretting such a tragic loss,
The Bishop drops his shepherd's crook,
And nails his Maker to the cross.

threat to Allies from Saddam's unexploded civilians

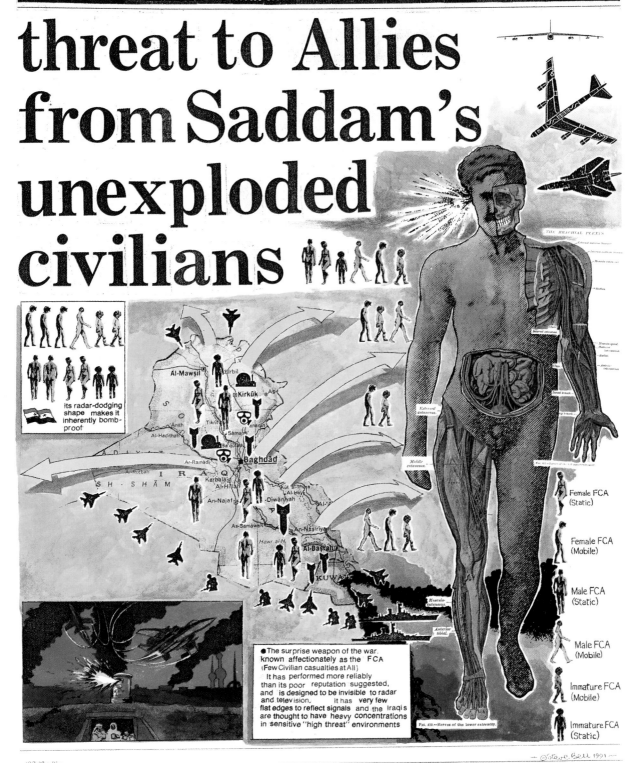

its radar-dodging shape makes it inherently bomb-proof

● The surprise weapon of the war, known affectionately as the FCA (Few Civilian casualties at All)
It has performed more reliably than its poor reputation suggested, and is designed to be invisible to radar and television. It has very few flat edges to reflect signals and the Iraqis are thought to have heavy concentrations in sensitive "high threat" environments

Female FCA (Static)

Female FCA (Mobile)

Male FCA (Static)

Male FCA (Mobile)

Immature FCA (Mobile)

Immature FCA (Static)

Panamania

I have a dream
That one day an American president
Will rise up and say to the world,
We hold certain lies to be self-evident,
That when we invade small countries
For the alleged purpose of saving democracy,
No one will take us seriously,
Apart, of course, from a British prime minister.

I have a dream
That a leader in the White House,
Who backs the world's biggest butchers
From China and Cambodia to the Americas,
To defend the bucks he holds most dear,
Will talk of life and liberty under God
With hand on heart,
And will keep a straight face.

Well, we can all dream...